When I Build with Blocks

by

Niki Alling

For all the Pre-K builders I've known through the years -
Your block structures are amazing!

For Freddy & Bless
Keep building your dreams.
I love you

I choose the block area, almost every day.

When I build with blocks, I can be anything.

I can build a royal castle where I am the King.

I can zoom in a rocket
to outer space.

I am a race car driver.
I can go very fast.

I have a race car
built to last!

zoom!

I am a firefighter,
I put out fires.

I build a fire truck
with a ladder and big tires.

I am an engineer
on a long train.

We build a giant fort,
to make sure the coast is clear.

I love to be a pilot,
and take my plane out for a flight.

I build a sprawling airport,
to land it for the night.

Castle

Rocket

Pirate Ship

Haunted House

Racecar

Fire Truck

Train

Bridge

Fort

Airport

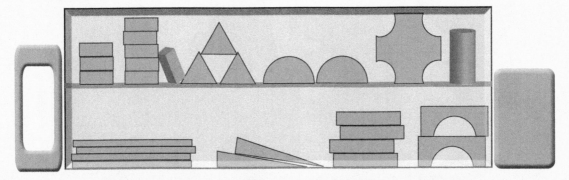

What will you build?

Special Thank You to:
Steve Anagnostos, Bessie Miller
and the children of Mr. Steve's Pre-K Class
For their support and fun ideas in the classroom!

Niki Alling, is the author and illustrator of several children's books, sci-fi time travel, paranormal short stories, popular everyday poetry for gifts, and more. She is a graphic designer and has been a paraprofessional in Pre-K for fifteen years. When I Build With Blocks, inspired by her Pre-K students, is fast becoming a classroom favorite with imaginative block builders and teachers.

When she's not writing, illustrating or working with children, she's busy having fun with her own grandchildren; hiking, fishing, blowing bubbles or building giant snowmen, in the beautiful Finger Lakes area of central New York.

Also by Niki Alling

Children's Books:
How Do You Peel A Banana?
The Straight Rainbow
The Roots of My Family Tree
Your Mother's Love
Your Father's Love
It's A Colorful Christmas
Hearts Are For Loving

Poetry:
Ants in My Snow Pants – Children's Poems Ebook
Reach – Inspirational Poetry Ebook
(Numerous Poems for cards & gifts, sold online at NikiClix Creations)

OTHER BOOKS BY NIKI ALLING:
Ginny's Sacrifice – Time Travel Novella

To learn more please visit:
Niki Alling's Blog
http://www.nikialling.com

CPSIA information can be obtained at www.ICGtesting.com
Printed in the USA
BVOW07*1146280915

419293BV00022B/43/P